BYRON

B Y R O N

THE REDE LECTURE FOR 1924

By

HERBERT HENSLEY HENSON, D.D.

*Hon. D.D. Glasgow and Durham
Sometime Fellow of All Souls
College, Oxford, Lord
Bishop of Durham*

CAMBRIDGE
AT THE UNIVERSITY PRESS
1924

CAMBRIDGE
UNIVERSITY PRESS

University Printing House, Cambridge CB2 8BS, United Kingdom

Cambridge University Press is part of the University of Cambridge.

It furthers the University's mission by disseminating knowledge in the pursuit of education, learning and research at the highest international levels of excellence.

www.cambridge.org
Information on this title: www.cambridge.org/9781316612460

© Cambridge University Press 1924

First published 1924
First paperback edition 2016

A catalogue record for this publication is available from the British Library

ISBN 978-1-316-61246-0 Paperback

BYRON

I

THE Bibliography which Professor Chew has appended to his laborious account of Byron's "fame and after-fame" fills no less than fifty-four rather closely-printed pages. This may serve to indicate the extent of the literature which has grown up around the name of Lord Byron. Its scale and variety attest the persistently alluring interest of the man, the range of his appeal, and the versatility of his genius. Moreover there is no reason for thinking that the magnetism of Byron is exhausted. The centenary of his death has occasioned a fresh output of articles, speeches, essays, appreciations, lectures, and even substantial volumes, which will add considerably to the mass of Byronic literature.

When the Vice-Chancellor honoured me with an invitation to deliver the

" Rede " lecture it seemed to me evidently suitable that I should choose as my theme the poet of world-resounding fame, whose name has its place in the great record of Cambridge, and whose death in Greece a hundred years ago in tragic circumstances thrilled Europe with compassionate and mournful homage.

Not indeed that I can add anything to the knowledge of his life, or to the understanding of his character. Everything worth knowing of the first is almost certainly known : every conceivable estimate of the last has most probably been presented. All I can hope to do is to direct attention to some aspects of both, and to add yet one more personal appreciation to the accumulated mass.

Lord Ernle, better known in the world of literature as Mr R. E. Prothero, the editor of the standard edition of Byron's *Letters and Journals*, has warned us against an impressionist treatment of the poet's career. That career, he says with truth, " lends itself only too easily to that method of treatment, which dashes off a likeness by vigorous strokes with a full brush, seizing with false emphasis on some salient feature, and revelling in striking contrasts of light and shade." He claims that in his letters Byron has painted his own portrait, and suggests that we may accept that portrait as a trustworthy presentation of the original:

"With slow, laborious touches, with delicate gradation of colour, sometimes with almost tedious minuteness and iteration, the gradual growth of a strangely composite character is presented, surrounded by the influences which controlled or moulded its development, and traced through all the varieties of its rapidly changing moods. Written, as Byron wrote, with habitual exaggeration, and on the impulse of the moment, his letters correct one another, and, from this point of view, every letter adds something to the truth and completeness of the portrait[1]."

Without dissenting from this estimate of the value of these fascinating compositions—they are confessedly among the best Letters in the language—it must be remembered that Byron was so impulsive and *impish* that it is never quite easy to determine how far his intentions or serious beliefs can be inferred from his

[1] v. *The Works of Lord Byron*, Vol. i. "Letters and Journals," ed. R. E. Prothero. 1922. Preface, p. viii.

words. He set down "anything that came uppermost," and was quite consciously whimsical and self-contradictory:

"This Journal is a relief"—he wrote in 1813[1] —"When I am tired—as I generally am—out comes this, and down goes everything. But I can't read it over; and God knows what contradictions it may contain. If I am sincere with myself (but I fear one lies more to one's self than to any one else), every page should confute, refute, and utterly abjure its predecessor."

A little later he gives this account of his political opinions, which is worth keeping in mind when his violent denunciations of particular politicians are considered:

"As for me, by the blessing of indifference, I have simplified my politics into an utter detestation of all existing governments; and, as it is the shortest and most agreeable and summary feeling imaginable, the first moment of an universal republic would convert me into an advocate for single and uncontradicted despotism. The fact is, riches are power, and poverty is slavery all over the earth, and one sort of establishment is no better nor worse for a *people* than another. I shall adhere to my party, because it would not be honourable to act otherwise; but as to *opinions*, I don't

[1] v. *Letters*, ii. 366.

think politics *worth* an *opinion*. *Conduct* is another thing:—if you begin with a party, go on with them. I have no consistency, except in politics: and *that* probably arises from my indifference on the subject altogether[1]."

Moreover there is no reason for thinking that Byron himself was not fully conscious of the literary charm of his letters. He could not be ignorant of the general interest which his biography would command, and he took some steps to facilitate its production by preparing the Memoirs, which were unfortunately destroyed after his death, and by indicating the sources from which his letters could be recovered[2]. It is not wholly easy to decide how far the careless ease and reckless self-disclosure of the letters indicate the frankness of unconsidering sincerity, and how far they may express a deliberate literary purpose. Nevertheless, when every allowance has been made, and every caution taken, I must needs hold with Lord Ernle that the Letters and Journals, read as a whole,

[1] v. *Letters*, II. 381.
[2] v. Letter to Murray, Sept. 28, 1821. (*Works, Letters and Journals*, ed. Prothero, Vol. v. p. 378.)

provide the best materials we possess for forming a trustworthy estimate of an enigmatic and fascinating personality.

In the long gallery of English poets the portrait of LORD BYRON is, perhaps, the most arresting. Every constituent of human interest met in his career: no element of moral paradox was lacking in his strangely mingled character. The violent oscillations of fortune which marked his life have been paralleled by the changing phases of his posthumous reputation. There have been those, the most eminent of his contemporaries, who held it not extravagant to set his poems beside the immortal productions of Shakespeare and Milton: there have been others, farther removed from the magic of his personality, who have challenged his right to be accounted a poet at all. The character of the man has been as hotly debated and as variously appraised as the quality of his work. Nothing has been normal, balanced, or discriminating where Byron has been concerned. Critics and admirers alike seem to lie under the necessity of speaking in superlatives. Of

no other poet can it be said that his life
is the indispensable gloss on his verse.
But Byron's poetry is never impersonal,
for Byron was absorbingly interesting
to himself. A monstrous and morbid
egotism is the key to his life, and
gives colour and passion to his poems.

The circumstances of his early life
stimulated this unwholesome trait, while
they deprived him of the disciplines
which might have checked and restrained
it. He was unhappy in both his parents.
His father was a worthless and heartless
rake: his mother one of the silliest of
women. John Byron died, "possibly by
his own hand," when his son was but
little more than three years old, so that
the task of the boy's upbringing fell to
his silly mother. He was subjected to
alternations of doting fondness, which
fostered his vanity, and vulgar abuse,
which moved his scorn. He was naturally an affectionate child, and would have
responded to kindness, but his mother's
folly was incredible. Her faults strength-
ened his. His personal vanity and absurd
pride of ancestry were inherited from

her, as well as his violent temper and erratic moods.

The prospect of social greatness was soon upheld before the child's eager eyes. If he can hardly be said to have been "born in the purple," for he was six years old before his cousin's death in 1794 made him heir to a peerage, and his great-uncle, "the wicked Lord Byron," refused to interest himself in his heir-apparent, yet the pride which is one of the worst consequences of that condition was not lessened, perhaps it was increased, by his actual indigence. On May 19, 1798, the sinister old man died, and the boy of ten succeeded to the title and estates. The flattery of inferiors, and the deference everywhere at that time shown to an English peer, albeit youthful, or undistinguished, or even contemptible, assisted the ill-effect of his ill-ordered home, and even the club-foot, which he so deeply resented, told in the same direction. It kept his attention fastened on himself, developed a self-conscious-ness which was always excessive, and led him unconsciously to emphasize other physical traits which were more agreeable to contemplate. The low tastes and fondness for the society of his inferiors which marked Byron in later years may have had their origin in, or at least have received disastrous encouragement from, the untoward circumstances of his boyhood. The well-known story of Byron, when no more than eleven years old, hurling a shell at Lord Portsmouth's head because he had playfully pinched his ear, and repudiating the suggestion that the missile was not intended for the head it had so narrowly missed—"But I *did* mean it ! I will teach a fool of an earl to pinch another noble's ear"— carries its own suggestion of precocious self-importance, and lack of discipline. Then followed Harrow, where though his house-master complained of his "inattention to business, and his propensity to make others laugh and disregard their employments as much as himself," he made some lasting friendships, read widely, and developed rapidly. Writing in 1821, he dwells on the remarkable range of his reading:

"Till I was eighteen years old (odd as it may seem), I had never read a review. But, while at Harrow, my general information was so great on modern topics, as to induce a suspicion that I could only collect so much information from *reviews*, because I was never *seen* reading, but always idle and in mischief, or at play. The truth is that I read eating, read in bed, read when no one else reads; and had read all sorts of reading since I was five years old, and yet never *met* with a review, which is the only reason that I know of why I should not have read them. But it is true; for I remember when Hunter and Curzon, in 1804, told me this opinion at Harrow, I made them laugh by my ludicrous astonishment in asking them, '*what is* a review?' To be sure, they were then less common. In three years more, I was better acquainted with that same, but the first I ever read was in 1806–7[1]."

Thus his neglect of his proper studies went along with an eager pursuit of the kind of knowledge he liked. "The moment I could read, my grand passion was *history*." A keen interest in affairs and great practical ability marked him throughout his career. In this respect, and not in this only, he may be compared with an earlier poet, whose character had many points of likeness to his own. Sir Philip Sidney (1554–1586) shared with

---

[1] v. *Letters and Journals*, v. 452.

Lord Byron the privilege of high birth, precocious genius, early and great popularity. He too was closely associated with foreign politics, and dedicated himself to a great European cause. What protestantism was to the Elizabethan poet, national liberty was to the Georgian. Both died for their faith. The one was the martyr of Dutch independence, the other of Greek. Zutphen may stand with Missolonghi in the record of Freedom. Both poets enjoyed great fame while they lived, and a posthumous reputation which has depended more on themselves than on their writings. But the difference is hardly less considerable than the resemblance, for while Sir Philip Sidney embodied the highest ideals of a chivalrous and religious age, Byron sank below the level of a generation which, so far as private morality is concerned, was neither exalted nor exacting. His personal record in this respect suggests inevitably the name of another earlier poet, strangely like himself in type and fortune. Wilmot, Earl of Rochester (1647–1680) also possessed the advantage of noble birth, and a rare satiric genius. But he too sank into an early grave under the burden of his own vices, and perhaps we may add that he too made a good end. Such parallels are, perhaps, more interesting than illuminating. The union of high literary gifts and practical sagacity is not infrequent. In Byron it was conspicuously illustrated. There is ever present in him, along with so much that is extravagant, morbid, and paradoxical, a practical shrewdness which would have been notable in any career, and is astonishing in his. Whether he be writing to Hanson and Kinnaird about his interminable financial affairs, or arranging with Murray for the publishing of his poems, or fomenting a rising in Italy, or negociating with the leaders of the Greek factions, he ever discloses a business capacity and strength of will which might seem little congruous with his temperament and habits. "Singular," wrote Scott in his Diary with reference to Byron's behaviour in Greece, "that a man whose conduct in his own personal affairs had been anything but practical, should be thus able to stand by the helm of a sinking state." But it was the dominance of untamed passions, not the absence of practical ability that worked the mischief in Byron's private affairs. He could have excelled in any way of life which he had brought himself to accept. Byron is never obscure or far-fetched. The directness of the man of action comes out in his style. He gives expression to reflections which occur to ordinary minds, and weaves into his verse knowledge that is the common heritage of moderately educated men. The enormous and continuing popularity of his poetry arises very largely from its intelligibility, and from the simplicity and obviousness of his themes. Nature, history, and social life always present the same wonders, tragedies and paradoxes. Byron utters magnificently the thoughts of "the man in the street." If he ever seriously meditated a parliamentary career, he appears soon to have abandoned the idea. He was too poor : he could not domesticate himself sufficiently in any party camp : he did not "bear fools gladly." On March

26th, 1813, he writes thus to Mrs Leigh:

"My parliamentary schemes are not much to my taste, I spoke twice last Session, and was told it was well enough; but I hate the thing altogether, and have no intention to 'strut another hour' on that stage. I am thus wasting the best part of my life daily repenting and never amending[1]."

Plainly he was, as the common saying goes, "at a loose end," and in obvious danger of "going to pieces." His sudden and complete triumph as an author carried him finally outside the range of parliamentary ambitions. Even the star of Scott paled before his rising sun. But his life was becoming embarrassed by his extravagance, and perilously discredited by his intrigues. A way of escape from both seemed to have opened when, on January 2nd, 1815, he was married to Miss Milbanke at Seaham. In fact, he had made the crowning error of his life. It is difficult to imagine a more hopelessly incongruous union, or a matrimonial failure more prolific of scandal. After a year of restless partnership Byron and his wife separated never to meet

[1] v. *Letters*, II. 197.

again. As if relieved from an incapacitating burden, his genius expressed itself with a power and altitude, of which even his previous achievements had hardly suggested the possibility. All his greater works were written after his flight from England in April 1816. But his self-respect was fatally wounded, and he drifted into a profligacy abroad which seemed to authenticate the worst calumnies at home. Byron sank to his lowest depth where his wife was concerned. On any view, he had sinned against her grossly. The least that could have been expected from him was a respectful reticence. But the wound to his vanity was too great, and he allowed himself to talk freely against his wife to strangers, to satirize her brutally in his poems, and to pose as the victim of her perverse and almost incomprehensible malignity. He had always been an impossible husband: he now ceased to carry himself as a gentleman. It is an aspect of Byron's career which no casuistry can justify, and no partiality condone.

II

THE two great compositions—*Childe Harold* and *Don Juan*—on which Byron's poetic reputation is securely based, are constructed on the same plan. Both are travel-epics in which the traveller's experiences are made the occasion for the author's reflections on men and things. In the one the journey lies through the scenery of nature and the sites of history. In the other it passes over the continent of life in society. Social "situations" take the place of historic scenes, and moralization takes the form of satire. The plan was both original and well-chosen. Mr Coleridge does not exaggerate the "originality of design" which Byron displayed:

"Childe Harold's Pilgrimage had no progenitors, and, with the exception of some feeble and forgotten imitations, it has had no descendants. The materials of the poem; the Spenserian stanza, suggested, perhaps, by Campbell's *Gertrude of Wyoming*, as well as by older models; the language, the metaphors, often appropriated and sometimes stolen from the Bible, from Shakespeare, from the classics; the

sentiments and reflections coeval with reflection and
sentiment, wear a familiar hue; but the poem itself,
a pilgrimage to scenes and cities of renown, a song
of travel, a rhythmical diorama, was Byron's own
handiwork—not an inheritance, but a creation[1]."

The plan was as well-chosen, as it was
original. The early nineteenth century
was a travelling age. For more than
a generation of almost unceasing war
England had been shut off from the continent. When, at length Peace restored
intercourse, the multitudes of English
tourists who crossed the Channel carried
abroad with them fresh eyes and a de-
vouring curiosity. *Childe Harold* was an
incomparable *vade mecum*. Moreover,
that was a moralizing age. The bitter
experience of war had set men thinking.
Questions going to the roots of every
convention, were clamouring for answer.
Authority, sacred and secular, had received in the Revolution a blow from
which no military and diplomatic
triumphs could enable it to recover.
There was the usual reaction after a
protracted strain, the inevitable collapse

[1] v. *Works*, ed. E. H. Coleridge, Vol. II., Introduction,
p. xiii.

after prolonged tension. The reckless
dissipation of the Few proceeded almost
confessedly in presence of the restless
misery of the Many. The world on
which the Genius of Byron broke forth
in sudden splendour was in the mood to
welcome the sombre scepticism of his
Pilgrim, and half-disposed to share his
listless disillusionment.

The method matched exactly the poet's
genius. "It was the instinct of Byron,"
observes Mr Bagehot, "*to give in glaring
words the gross phenomena of evident ob-
jects.*" This is true if for the belittling
adjective "glaring" we substitute, as in
justice we ought, "felicitous," "beautiful," and "stately." Byron's mind was
curiously concrete. His power of mani-
pulating material was matchless, but his
imagination was comparatively feeble,
and his initiative small. His poems re-
flect his reading, his journeys, his personal
experiences, his moods. His letters and
diaries are a running commentary on the
poetry. He had little capacity for sus-
tained thought, but his interest was ab-
sorbing while it held, his vision was

keen, and his impressions found imme-
diate expression in language of extraordinary force and felicity. What he had
seen he could recall with exactness, and
describe with eloquence and beauty.
What he had read, he could remember
and utilize. What he had felt, he could
utter with rare force and feeling. But
always his poetry is descriptive of something he has seen, or read, or felt. It is
tied fast to a definite datum on which it
can work. His fancy never left the earth.
He lived in no visionary world like
Shelley, nor could he like Wordsworth
interpret and canonize Nature: but he
could picture with an almost photographic
fidelity, and bring into his verse all the
treasures of his knowledge and experience.
Southey, in his *Vision of Judgment*, pro-
vided the instrument of his own un-
doing, for Byron accepted the suggestion
and fashioned it to the service of his
vindictive purpose. Lucifer is a poor
attenuated modernized reproduction of
Milton's Satan. Of the famous description of the shipwreck in the 2nd Canto
of *Don Juan*, he wrote "that there was

not a single circumstance of it not taken
from fact; not, indeed, from any single
shipwreck, but all from actual facts of
different wrecks." Nothing was im-
agined: everything was reproduced from
his reading. "Norman Abbey" in the
13th Canto is Newstead described in
great detail, and with astonishing ac-
curacy from his memory of it:

"The Mansion's self was vast and venerable,
  With more of the monastic than has been
Elsewhere preserved; the cloisters still were stable,
  The cells, too, and Refectory, I ween:
An exquisite small chapel had been able,
  Still unimpaired, to decorate the scene;
The rest had been reformed, replaced, or sunk,
  And spoke more of the baron than the monk."

It is impossible to separate the personality of Byron from his poetry. His
enormous egotism clothed every personal
experience with such importance in his
eyes that he uttered it inevitably in his
verse. It is this circumstance which
gives such importance to the miserable
problem which his grandson claimed to
have solved by the publication of *Astarte*.
If, as cannot be disputed, his conduct is
the key to his verse, may not his verse

be the key to his conduct? If there be such a measure of ambiguity in the letters as may permit a verdict of "non proven," may not the indirect witness of *Manfred* turn the scale, and compel the sterner conclusion? "The *motif* of Manfred is remorse—eternal suffering for inexpiable crime—Manfred is no echo of another's questioning, no expression of a general world-weariness on the part of the time-spirit, but a personal outcry 'De profundis clamavi!'" If Mr Coleridge is right then the drama had its origin in the author's actual behaviour, and we must needs hold that Lord Lovelace achieved his purpose. Nor is this all. We must read other compositions of Byron in the light of our conclusion. The tender and beautiful *Epistle to Augusta* is seen to be charged with an intolerable eroticism, and the one instance of a pure affection for a woman holding Byron through life must be blotted out of the record. Many will feel that this is intolerable. They will point to his inveterate habit of exaggeration: to his "inverted hypocrisy"

which made him pose as worse than he
was: to the many circumstances which
seem to establish Mrs Leigh's innocence:
to the disposition to credit him with
everything that was monstrous. Perhaps,
as in the case of Mary Queen of Scots,
the decision will finally be determined
by considerations that find no admission
to the formal discussion.

The Satire of Byron was not inspired
by the *saeva indignatio* which burned in
the stern spirit of Swift, nor was it the
Puritanic scorn which filled the mind
of Juvenal, nor the flippant ribald enjoy-
ment of paradox which gleams from the
pages of Lucian and Voltaire. It also
was born of his personal experiences and
resentments. He had the disbelief in
human virtue which grows from a man's
own vices: he felt the repugnance and
bitterness which a condemned felon feels
against his comrades who have given
evidence against him. Underneath his
verse the reader feels, not a zeal for
righteousness, but a repudiation of moral
law. It is the cynical talk of the smoking-
room elevated by genius into great lite-

rature which *Don Juan* exhibits, not a
solemn indictment of social hypocrisy
springing from a passion for truth. There
is in it also that revenge which Lady
Byron regarded as the key to his marital
behaviour. He had fled from Society
with the vindictive feelings of a dis-
missed servant whose revenge takes the
form of calumnious gossip about his late
employers.

Byron, we know, was an incorrigible
poseur, and there was no pose which
attracted him more than that of the
Sensualist-hero, pictured with remarkable power and sympathy in *Sardanapalus*.
It was thus that he loved to picture himself to his own admiration, and, perhaps,
to alleviate the protests of his own self-
respect:

> "In his effeminate heart
> There is a careless courage which Corruption
> Has not all quenched, and latent energies,
> Repressed by circumstance, but not destroyed—
> Steeped, but not drowned, in deep voluptuousness.
> If born a peasant, he had been a man
> To have reached an empire: to an empire born,
> He will bequeath none; nothing but a name,
> Which his sons will not prize in heritage:—
> Yet—not all lost—even yet—he may redeem

His sloth and shame, by only being that
Which he should be, as easily as the thing
He should not be and is."

It is the familiar sophistry of the
sensualist—"the plausible casuistry of
the passions," as Jeremy Taylor calls it—
which Byron places in the mouth of the
Assyrian monarch when he justifies himself to his Mentor:

" 'Tis true I have not shed
Blood as I might have done, in oceans, till
My name became the synonyme of Death—
A terror and a trophy. But for this
I feel no penitence; my life is love:
If I must shed blood, it shall be by force.
Till now, no drop from an Assyrian vein
Hath flowed for me—"

Byron was neither so effeminate, nor
so gentle as his hero. His life, though
disgraced by occasional excesses and for
a time sunk in a swinish self-indulgence,
was by no means one of unrelieved
sensuality. It was ordinarily marked by
abstemiousness, hard physical exertion,
and extraordinary mental activity. The
hectic vehemence of his writing is not
unconnected with the severity of his
asceticism in eating and drinking. Mr
Leslie Stephen's account of his habits

suggests the Spartan rather than the Epicurean:

"He now subsided into an indolent routine, to which he adhered with curious pertinacity. Trelawney describes the day at Pisa soon afterwards, and agrees with Moore, Hunt, Medwin, and Gamba. He rose very late, took a cup of green tea, had a biscuit and soda-water at two, rode out and practised shooting, dined most abstemiously, visited the Gambas in the evening, and returned to read or write till two or three in the morning. At Ravenna previously and afterwards in Greece he kept nearly to the same hours. His rate of composition at this period was surprising. Medwin says that after sitting with Byron till two or three the poet would next day produce fresh work[1]."

Mr Leslie Stephen calls this "an indolent routine," but the description is perhaps marked by something less than his usual felicity.

In spite of the kindness with which he treated his servants, his evident dislike of inflicting physical pain, his facile motions of generosity, and the strength of his attachment to his friends, Byron included in his strangely blended character elements of cynicism and cruelty which stain his personal record. His whole treatment of Allegra's mother was marked

[1] v. *Dictionary of National Biography*, Article "Byron."

by coldness of heart and a harshness not far removed from brutality, nor was his behaviour to the poor child all that might have been expected from a just and considering father. If it must be allowed that Lady Caroline Lamb was infinitely provoking, still his final dismissal of the foolish creature whose infatuation he had certainly encouraged, was offensively and gratuitously heartless. Nor is his relation with the Shelleys unshadowed by surprising meannesses. Even if we accept Mr Murray's generous effort to purge from his memory the foul stain of suppressing Mrs Shelley's defence of her husband against the calumnies which Hoppner had reported to Byron, it remains true that he credited without protest the most infamous charges against one whom he called his friend, and professed to admire.

This vein of cruelty comes out in his satire, a circumstance which may, perhaps, be explained by the fact that his victims were generally those whom he regarded as personal enemies. Even the Prince-Regent, though a poor creature

enough however viewed, hardly merited
the savage spite with which Byron pur-
sued him. His immorality was indeed
shameless, but not so aggressively shameless as that of his critic; and if, in the
critic's case, a generous mind will allow
large extenuations in the unwisdom of
his upbringing and the demoralizing
circumstances in which he lived, these
on no smaller scale can also be pleaded
in the monarch's. To both men marriage
brought a special infamy, but of the two
Byron was certainly not the least infamous. George IV's political blunders
were shared by the most eminent of his
subjects, and his personal behaviour was
not without redeeming touches of kindness, intelligence, and even magnanimity.
It is to the credit of both that they won
and kept the regard of Sir Walter Scott.
But Byron's indifference to justice in his
treatment of individuals was notorious.
His facile pen would eulogize or scarify
at choice, and the choice might be determined by some quite trivial personal
incident. His judgment was ever the
slave of his resentments, and the violence

of his feelings found such easy expression in his verse that he wrote for the mere pleasure of writing. He knew his power, and how easily a slight personal irritation would lead him to use it. "If I took you all in hand," he wrote pleasantly to Murray (Sept. 24th, 1821), "it would not be difficult to cut you up like gourds. I did as much by as powerful people at nineteen years old, and I know little as yet, in three-and-thirty, which should prevent me from making all your ribs Gridirons for your hearts if such were my propensity." It was indeed prophetic of Byron's satiric method that his savage onslaught on Lord Carlisle—

> "No Muse will cheer, with renovating smile
> The paralytic puling of Carlisle—"

was actually substituted for some flattering lines because the Earl had not presented him on taking his seat in the House of Lords! It is a curious but inevitable question whether Byron's attitude towards Wordsworth would not have been different if he had known that Wordsworth disapproved the review of *Hours of Idleness* in the *Edinburgh*.

"Here is a young man, a lord," he said, "who has published a little volume of verse; and these fellows attack him, as if no one may write poetry unless he lives in a garret. The young man will do something, if he goes on." Byron and Wordsworth were of course mutually antipathetic, but the younger poet knew the greatness of the elder, and was more influenced by him than he realized.

Southey may be said to have earned his fate: but Coleridge deserved better treatment at Byron's hands. His relations with Scott are, perhaps, the most honourable, as those with Thomas Moore are the most affectionate of his literary friendships. The connection between the two poets had opened inauspiciously with Byron's attack on Scott in *English Bards and Scotch Reviewers* (1809) in which the "Wizard of the North" had been held up to opprobrium as "Apollo's venal son." Scott, the least venal of men, naturally resented the description.

"It is funny enough," he wrote, "to see a whelp of a young Lord Byron abusing me, of whose circumstances he knows nothing, for endeavouring to scratch

out a living with my pen. God help the bear, if, having
little else to eat, he must not even suck his own
paws. I can assure the noble imp of fame it is not
my fault that I was not born to a park and £5000
a year, as it is not his lordship's merit, although it
may be his great good fortune, that he was not born
to live by his literary talents or success[1]."

Scott admired *Childe Harold*, but dis-
liked its tone, which he thought con-
ceited and unwholesome. It was, he
wrote to Morritt, "upon the whole a
piece of most extraordinary power, and
may rank its author with our first poets."
By Murray's judicious intervention the
two poets were brought together. Scott
explained "the circumstances respecting
the sale of *Marmion*" which Byron had
misrepresented, and received the frankest
expression of regret. "The Satire," said
Byron, "was written when I was very
young and very angry and fully bent on
displaying my wrath and my wit, and
now I am haunted by the ghosts of my
wholesale assertions." He proceeded to
flatter Scott's pride by retailing the com-
pliments which the Prince Regent had

[1] v. Lockhart's *Life of Scott*, II. 83.

paid to his poetry. The acquaintance
passed quickly into a genuine mutual regard. Byron's poetry speedily displaced
Scott's in the public regard—"Byron hits
the mark where I don't even pretend to
fledge my arrow" was the older poet's
generous comment. Lockhart held that
"Byron owed at least half his success to
clever though perhaps unconscious imi-
tation of Scott, and no trivial share of the
rest to the lavish use of materials which
Scott never employed, only because his
genius was, from the beginning to the end
of his career under the guidance of high
and chivalrous feelings of moral rectitude[1]."
Undoubtedly no one could ever have said
of Byron what the Bishop of Durham
could, with universal agreement, say of
Scott, "that everything he had written
tended to the practice of virtue, and to
the improvement of the human race."
But the poetry of both Scott and Byron
owed what popularity it gained to a
phase of feeling which was quickly out-
passed. It was not as a romantic poet
that either of them was destined to rise to

[1] v. *Life of Scott*, ii. 509.

his full height. Byron's estimate of Scott's work was generous and discriminating.

"Scott is certainly the most wonderful writer of the day. His novels are a new literature in themselves, and his poetry as good as any—and only ceased to be so popular, because the vulgar learned were tired of hearing 'Aristides called the Just' and Scott the Best, and ostracised him[1]."

Byron's admiration of the *Waverley Novels* was unbounded. He insisted on having them sent to him as they appeared, read them again and again, quoted them incessantly, and never wearied of praising them. For Scott himself he expressed the utmost respect. To Scott he dedicated *Cain*, and was perhaps as much surprised as delighted that he accepted the dedication. Mr Edgcumbe has bracketed Scott with Shelley as the only two of his contemporaries whom Byron "admired[2]." It is, perhaps, true to say that Scott was the only one whom he respected. In 1823 Byron wrote to Henri Beyle ("Stendhal") a protest against a slighting reference which he had made in a pamphlet to Scott's character. We may take this as his deliberate estimate of the man:

[1] v. *Letters*, v. 167.   [2] v. *Byron, the last Phase*, p. 35.

"You say that 'his (Scott's) character is little worthy of enthusiasm,' at the same time that you mention his productions in the manner they deserve. I have known Walter Scott long and well, and in occasional situations which call forth the *real* character—and I can assure you that his character *is* worthy of admiration, that of all men he is the most *open*, the most *honourable*, the most *amiable*. With his politics I have nothing to do: they differ from mine, which renders it difficult for me to speak of them. But he is *perfectly sincere* in them: and Sincerity may be humble, but she cannot be servile. I pray you, therefore, to correct or soften that passage. You may, perhaps, attribute this officiousness of mine to a false affectation of *candour*, as I happen to be a writer also. Attribute it to what motive you please, but *believe the truth*. I say that Walter Scott is as nearly a thorough good man as man can be, because I *know* it by experience to be the case[1]."

In the numerous references to Scott scattered through Byron's letters there is nothing inconsistent with the opinions here expressed. They are as honourable to the author of the eulogy as to its subject.

Byron's Ravenna Diary was sent by Murray to Scott, to whom it suggested the plan of keeping a similar record of occasional reflexions. Thus we owe to the younger poet that illuminating and pathetic composition, *Sir Walter Scott's*

[1] v. *Letters*, etc., VI. 220.

Journal, which has a place of its own in the literature of self-revelation. Captain Basil Hall is quoted by Lockhart as the authority for some notable observations on Byron made by Scott in 1825 when the memory of Byron's death was yet recent.

" He (Byron) quoted, with the bitterest despair to Scott the strong expression of Shakespeare:

> The gods are just, and of our pleasant vices
> Make instruments to scourge us;"

and added, "I would to God that I could have your peace of mind, Mr Scott; I would give all I have, all my fame, everything, to be able to speak on this subject" (that of domestic happiness) "as you do."

Sir Walter describes Byron as being a man of real goodness of heart, and the kindest and best feelings, miserably thrown away by his foolish contempt of public opinion. Instead of being warned or checked by public opposition, it roused him to go on in a worse strain:

"Many, many a pleasant hour I have spent with him", Sir Walter added, "And I never met a man with nobler feelings, or one who, had he not unfortunately taken the wrong course, might have done more to make himself beloved and respected. A man of eminence in any line, and perhaps a man of great literary eminence especially, is exposed to a thousand eyes which men, not so celebrated, are safe from—and, in consequence, right conduct is much more essential to his happiness than to those who are less watched: and I may add, that only by such conduct can the permanence of his real influence over any class be secured. I could not persuade Byron to see it in this light—the more's the pity, for he had no justice done him[1]."

It was good advice, and kindly meant, but there was that in Byron's personal record, which possibly Scott may have suspected though could not certainly know, which closed for him the path of moral sanity in which he was counselled to walk. And the malady which, in Scott's opinion, "tinctured some part of this mighty genius" may have gone deeper than "the two peculiarities of extreme suspicion and love of mischief" which he had observed[2].

[1] v. Lockhart's *Life of Scott*, IV. 218.
[2] v. *Sir Walter Scott's Journal*, I. 12.

III

WHAT was Byron's personal religion? The question has been much discussed, and can hardly be avoided. That religion was extremely interesting to him is apparent: that some aspects of current Christianity moved his dislike and contempt is notorious: that other, and perhaps more important aspects, attracted him appears to be certain. He has been often represented as the victim of the crude Calvinism of his Presbyterian nurse. Writing to Gifford (June 18th, 1813) Byron disclaims the character of an infidel, and suggests that his scepticism was to be interpreted as a reaction from the severity of his religious training in childhood:

"I am no Bigot to Infidelity, and did not expect that, because I doubted the immortality of Man, I should be charged with denying the existence of a God. It was the comparative insignificance of ourselves and *our world*, when placed in competition with the mighty whole, of which it is an atom, that first led me to imagine our pretensions to eternity might be overrated.

This, and being early disgusted with a Calvinistic
Scotch school, where I was cudgelled to Church for
the first ten years of my life, afflicted me with this
malady; for, after all, it is, I believe, a disease of the
mind as much as other kinds of hypochondria."

This explanation of his irreligion,
though certainly not negligible, has been,
perhaps, over-emphasized. It is suggested that, if the brilliant and sensitive
child had been brought under the influence of a gentler and brighter creed,
the spiritual catastrophe of later life
might have been averted. We are bidden
to see in the libertine poet a notable
illustration of that terrible condition
which the XVIIth Article describes as
the effect of an undue insistence on Predestination in the case of "curious and
carnal persons." It is assuredly true that
Byron was both curious and carnal, and
his life in London, and Venice, might
not inaptly be summed up in the for-
midable phrase of the Anglican Con-
fession "wretchlessness of most unclean
living." But there was much more in
Byron's career than this, and at most the
description holds good of a phase, and
not the principal phase, of a many-phased

life. Byron was undoubtedly trained in a
crudely literal understanding of the Bible,
and it may well be the case that with
him, as with many others, this literalism
hindered his appreciation of Christianity
in later years. But the exact knowledge
of the Scriptures which he acquired as
a child, and the continued interest in
them which he showed as a man, were
circumstances not in themselves un-
favourable to personal religion. His wife,
writing many years after his death,
assured H. C. Robinson that he had been
"a believer in the inspiration of the
Bible, and had the gloomiest Calvinistic
tenets," and to this cause she ascribed the
misery of his life. But Lady Byron was
temperamentally disqualified for understanding her husband, and her disqualifi-
cation did not diminish as she grew old.
The gloomy passages in his poems which
picture a belief or, rather, haunting dread
of predestination to evil need not be
understood as disclosing his personal
creed, and the Calvinistic dogma was
too serviceable a weapon in his continuing controversy with contemporary

Christianity not to be utilized to the full. There was, indeed, in Byron a strain of natural melancholy, which predisposed him to the sterner theology, and the disorders of his conduct bred in him a depressing sense of self-degradation which perhaps commended that theology by a private argument more powerful than reasonable. He may perhaps be numbered among those who must strive

> "with Demons who impair
> The strength of better thoughts, and seek their prey
> In melancholy bosoms—such as were
> Of moody texture from their earliest day,
> And loved to dwell in darkness and dismay
> Deeming themselves predestined to a doom
> Which is not of the pangs that pass away;
> Making the Sun like blood, the Earth a tomb,
> The tomb a hell—and Hell itself a murkier gloom."

Byron was a student of Voltaire, whose mordant profanity accorded but too well with his own contempt for conventionalized religion, but the two men had come into collision with established Christianity in very different ways. It could not be said of Byron, as the late Lord Morley said of Voltaire, that his attack on religion "was in the first instance prompted, and throughout its course stimulated and embittered, by antipathy to the external organisation of the religion." No powerful and persecuting institution confronted the Englishman of the nineteenth century as it confronted the Frenchman of the eighteenth. The Church of England in the time of the Prince-Regent lay open to many and grave charges, but intolerance was not among them. Not even the harshest critic would describe it as a "socially pestilent" system. Byron's revolt was against the least ecclesiastical version of the national Christianity. The fashionable Evangelicalism, against which he directed his sharpest gibes, was not prone to the exaltation of the hierarchy. Cant, against which Byron waged immitigable war, has always been the shadow of Evangelicalism. That version of Christianity was too emotional, too disdainful of intellect and beauty, too hostile to the gay intercourse of social life, to be agreeable, or, indeed, altogether intelligible, to a man of his temperament and quality. Of Wilberforce, the Saint of Evangelicalism he writes with genuine admiration, but the particular cause which Wilberforce espoused with such single-minded devotion was precisely that which accorded with the passion for liberty which was Byron's most honourable trait.

"O Wilberforce! thou man of black renown,
  Whose merit none enough can sing or say,
Thou hast struck one immense Colossus down,
  Thou moral Washington of Africa!
But there's another little thing, I own,
  Which you should perpetrate some summer's day
And set the other half of earth to rights;
  You have freed the *blacks*—now pray shut up the
    whites."

Cowper, whose powers both as a satirist and a letter writer were hardly inferior to his own, he describes as "that maniacal Calvinist and coddled poet"; a description which has but too much justification in a career shadowed by calamity and spoiled by mishandling. Byron was ill-placed for appreciating Christianity. If the impressions of his childhood were those of a harsh and gloomy creed, those of his youth and early manhood were neither morally exalting nor spiritually impres-

sive. The Church of England was not
seen to advantage in the public schools,
or in the universities, or in the fashionable world, or at the tables of the Whig
magnates, or in the clubs which Byron
frequented. Probably Harrow left on him
no better impression of clergymen than
Westminster had left on Cowper a few
years before, and if his conscience was
less sensitive than Cowper's, his insight
was as keen, and his will to criticize
stronger. His Cambridge contemporaries
who subsequently were ordained, though
respectable and cultivated men, were hardly well-qualified to commend Christianity
to the young peer, whose favours they
sought, and whose vanity they fostered.
Sydney Smith was an admirable wit, and
in his way an excellent parish clergyman,
but his conversation was not markedly
different from that of the Whig politicians, whose society he frequented, and
Byron's description of him does not indicate any unusual measure of respect:

"And lo! upon that day it came to pass,
　I sate next that o'erpowering son of Heaven,
The very powerful parson, Peter Pith,
　The loudest wit I e'er was deafened with.

I knew him in his livelier London days,
   A brilliant diner-out, though but a curate,
And not a joke he cut but earned its praise,
   Until Preferment, coming at a sure rate,
(O Providence! how wondrous are thy ways!
   Who would suppose thy gifts sometimes obdurate?)
Gave him, to lay the Devil who looks o'er Lincoln,
   A fat fen vicarage, and nought to think on.

His jokes were sermons, and his sermons jokes;
   But both were thrown away amongst the fens;
For Wit hath no great friends in aguish folks.
   No longer ready ears and short-hand pens
Imbibed the gay *bon-mot*, or happy hoax;
   The poor priest was reduced to common sense,
Or to coarse efforts very loud and long,
   To hammer a hoarse laugh from the thick throng."

There was nothing in Sydney Smith's blend of politics and religion to make either respect-worthy in Byron's eyes. Perhaps as Dr Johnson found the merriment of parsons "mighty offensive," and even the worldly-minded Pepys was scandalized by the profane proceedings at Archbishop Sheldon's table, Byron felt a certain repugnance to the social prominence of the witty parson at the Whig dinners. In judging his treatment of religion we have to remember that he never at any period of his career had been well-placed for appreciating it.

Byron, like many other libertines, was
fond of discussing religion. Partly, perhaps, this is to be explained as just one
more exhibition of his incorrigible youth-
fulness. It was only the undergraduate's
habit of arguing for arguing's sake which
had survived into later life. Partly, it
was his whimsical delight in the astonishment caused by his equipment for such
discussions—his unusual acquaintance
with the Bible, with the works of apo-
logetic divines, and with all the stock
objections to Christianity. Harness describes the "very serious discussions on
religion" in which Byron engaged his
guests Hodgson and himself at Newstead
in 1811:

"Byron, from his early education in Scotland, had
been taught to identify the principles of Christianity
with the extreme dogmas of Calvinism. His mind
had thus imbibed a most miserable prejudice, which
appeared to be the only obstacle to his hearty accept-
ance of the Gospel. Of this error we were most
anxious to disabuse him. The chief weight of the
argument rested with Hodgson, who was older a
good deal than myself[1]."

This debate was renewed in the last

[1] *Letters and Journals*, i. 179.

months of his life when the Scotch doctor,
Kennedy, amused the officers of the
British garrison at Argostoli by the fer-
vour with which he endeavoured to
convert Byron to his own Methodistical
creed. Mr Harold Nicolson, in his
admirable account of the last year of
Byron's life, has described the discussion
with characteristic humour; "And I,
for one," he concludes, "am of opinion
that in his conversations with Dr Kennedy Lord Byron was in no way guilty
of insincerity. For had the doctor been a
Catholic, and not a Methodist, the result
might well have been a dramatic and
emotional conversion[1]."

Would the religion of Italy have been
more congenial to him than the religion
of England? Would he have found it
easier to tolerate the intellectual servi-
tude of Rome than to sustain the intellectual squalor of Evangelicalism?
Would the Jesuit casuistry have been
less offensive than the "cant" of English
society? Would the enormous abuses of

[1] v. *Byron, the last Journey, April* 1823—*April* 1824, by
Harold Nicolson, p. 152. Constable and Co. 1924.

the Established Church have been out-
weighed by the shameless paradoxes of
the Roman system? It is hard to say.
Sir Walter Scott thought that, if ever
he reformed his ways, he would probably
"retreat upon the Catholic faith and dis-
tinguish himself by the austerity of his
penances[1]."

He wished his daughter to be a Roman Catholic, which he said, he "looked
upon as the best religion," and he sent
her to be educated in a convent. "I
think," he wrote to Moore (March 4th,
1822), "people can never have *enough* of
religion, if they are to have any." This
does not indicate a serious view of religion, but it may disclose a tendency[2].
It is conceivable that, if his life had been
prolonged, it might have included some
such dramatic conversion as that which
added the Founder of the Jesuits to the
Roman calendar, but it is not probable.
His heredity, temperament, intellect, and

---

[1] v. Lockhart's *Life of Scott*, Vol. II. p. 514.
[2] Cf. the letter of March 8th to Moore, where he disclaims flippancy and professes to be "a great admirer of
tangible religion." (v. *Letters*, VI. 38.)

habit suggest rather that he would have taken his own life in some ecstasy of intolerable self-disgust. It is certain that he often suffered his thought to dwell on this possibility, from which he was protected neither by a strong religious creed, nor by a high sense of duty, nor by any coercive private obligations. But this is mere speculation. What is certain is that he cast away his life very nobly in an honourable venture which adds a touch a nobility to his stained and shadowed career.

IV

BYRON's passion for liberty was deep and genuine. It was more than the political cant which inspired the rounded periods and purple perorations of the Whig orators. It is disclosed in the boy; it is paramount in the man. His incoherent disordered life finds a principle of continuity in his championship of the enslaved. It would, indeed, be a gross error to regard Byron as what is now

called a "democrat." Scott, an aristocrat
to the back-bone, judged him rightly to
be "a patrician on principle." All forms
of government seemed to him bad—so
far he felt with Shelley,—but democracy
was the worst of all. "For what," he
asks, "is democracy?" and he answers
tersely that it is "an Aristocracy of
Blackguards." He had no sympathy to
spare for the English agitators, Hunt and
Cobbett. In his view they were "such
infamous scoundrels" that they discredited any cause which they espoused.
They were only "very low imitations of
the Jacobins." "I protest," he wrote to
Hobhouse (April 22nd, 1820), "not
against *reform*, but my most thorough
contempt and abhorrence of all that I
have seen, read, or heard, of the persons
calling themselves *reformers*, *radicals*, and
such other names[1]." But if the faults of
peoples were ever clearly seen, the crimes
of their rulers were not less evident, and
even more repulsive. Indeed, he held the
crimes to be responsible for most of the
faults. Accordingly he would not be

[1] v. *Lord Byron's Correspondence*, ed. Murray, II. 143.

alienated from the Cause of Freedom by the servile incompetence of those who clamoured for it. The cowardice and treachery of the down-trodden Italians disgusted, but did not discourage, him:

"There are materials in this people, and a noble energy, if well directed. But who is to direct them? No matter. Out of such times heroes spring. Difficulties are the hotbeds of high spirits, and Freedom the mother of the few virtues incident to human nature[1]."

He rose above himself when he meditated on their wrongs, and was ready to embrace all risks on their behalf. Thus he reveals himself in his Diary (January 9th, 1821):

"I shall not fall back; though I don't think (the Italian insurgents) in force or heart sufficient to make much of it. But, *onward*!—it is now the time to act, and what signifies *self*, if a single spark of that which would be worthy of the past can be bequeathed unquenchedly to the future? It is not one man, nor a million, but the *spirit* of liberty which must be spread. The waves which dash upon the shore are, one by one, broken, but yet the *ocean* conquers, nevertheless. It overwhelms the Armada, it wears the rock, and, if the Neptunians are to be believed, it has not only destroyed, but made a world. In like manner, whatever the sacrifice of individuals, the great cause will gather strength, sweep down

[1] v. *Letters and Journals*, v. 161.

what is rugged, and fertilise (for *sea-weed* is *manure*) what is cultivable. And so, the mere selfish calculation ought never to be made on such occasions; and, at present, it shall not be computed by me. I was never a good arithmetician of chances, and shall not commence now[1]."

So with the still more down-trodden and therefore still more degraded Greeks. No one had clearer vision of their faults. He had written bitterly of them in *Childe Harold*. They were hoping to be enfranchised by the aid of the Christian Powers: Byron bade them trust to their own exertions:

"Hereditary Bondsmen! know ye not
　Who would be free *themselves* must strike the blow?
　By their right arms the conquest must be wrought?
　Will Gaul or Muscovite redress ye? No!
　True—they may lay your proud despoilers low,
　But not for you will Freedom's Altars flame.
　Shades of the Helots! triumph o'er your foe!
　Greece! change thy lords, thy state is still the
　　　same;
Thy glorious day is o'er, but not thine years of
　　　shame."

He appended to the poem a notable apology for the Greeks, which has perhaps not even yet lost value.

[1] v. *Letters*, v. 163.

"At present (i.e. 1810) like the Catholics of Ireland and the Jews throughout the world, and such other cudgelled and heterodox people, they (the Greeks) suffer all the moral and physical ills that can afflict humanity. Their life is a struggle against truth; they are vicious in their own defence. They are so unused to kindness, that when they occasionally meet with it they look upon it with suspicion, as a dog often beaten snaps at your fingers if you attempt to caress him. They are ungrateful, notoriously, abominably ungrateful!—this is the general cry. Now, in the Name of Nemesis! for what are they to be grateful? Where is the human being that ever conferred a benefit on Greek or Greeks? They are to be grateful to the Turks for their fetters, and to the Franks for their broken promises and lying counsels. They are to be grateful to the artist who engraves their ruins, and to the antiquary who carries them away; to the traveller whose janissary flogs them, and to the scribbler whose journal abuses them. This is the amount of their obligations to foreigners[1]."

Mr Harold Nicolson has re-told the history of Byron's last months with knowledge, eloquence, and discrimination. He claims to tell the truth "with that realism which Byron of all men, would have desired," and certainly his work cannot be accused of excessive sympathy or an undue indulgence in

[1] v. *Poetry*, II. 191.

natural sentiment. He exhibits a tangled and squalid story of meanness, stupidity, and fatuous vanity in which the steady purpose of the dying poet is almost the only relieving factor. He disallows the "legend that Byron went to Greece inspired solely by Philhellenic enthusiasms," and maintains that his sojourn in Missolonghi was only "a succession of humiliating failures." It may be answered that human motives are rarely unmingled, and that in the case of Byron his final venture for Greece stood in line with an interest which he had ever championed and served, and that if an unselfish purpose may ever be credited to a man it is hard to imagine how Byron's purpose can be excluded from the description. He gave his fortune with no sparing hand: he gave the relics of his strength: he held on when others flinched: he crowned his service by dying at his post. No admirer of Byron need quarrel with Mr Nicolson's estimate of what he effected:

"Lord Byron accomplished nothing at Missolonghi except his own suicide; but by that single act of heroism he secured the liberation of Greece. Had Byron, as he was urged, deserted the Hellenic cause in February 1824, there would I feel convinced, have been no Navarino: the whole history of South-eastern Europe would have developed differently."

If this be a just verdict, there is no exaggeration in describing Lord Byron as the Liberator of Greece, and he would have desired for himself no prouder title.

As to the man himself, with his amazing abilities, his vulgar vanity and magnanimous tolerance, his immense faults, his heights and depths of feeling, his incredible blunders, his achievements in word and deed, his triumphs, and failures, what can be said? Praise and blame are alike unfitting in presence of a career so enigmatic and so mighty. Give me leave to adapt his own words about his favourite among the ancients, Alcibiades, and apply them to himself:

"Yet upon the whole it may be doubted, whether there be a name of *modern* times which comes to us with such a general charm as that of Byron. Why? I cannot answer: who can?"

9 781316 612460